Collared Lemmings

by Rebecca Pettiford

BLASTOFF!
2
READERS

BELLWETHER MEDIA • MINNEAPOLIS, MN

Note to Librarians, Teachers, and Parents:

Blastoff! Readers are carefully developed by literacy experts and combine standards-based content with developmentally appropriate text.

Level 1 provides the most support through repetition of high-frequency words, light text, predictable sentence patterns, and strong visual support.

Level 2 offers early readers a bit more challenge through varied simple sentences, increased text load, and less repetition of high-frequency words.

Level 3 advances early-fluent readers toward fluency through increased text and concept load, less reliance on visuals, longer sentences, and more literary language.

Level 4 builds reading stamina by providing more text per page, increased use of punctuation, greater variation in sentence patterns, and increasingly challenging vocabulary.

Level 5 encourages children to move from "learning to read" to "reading to learn" by providing even more text, varied writing styles, and less familiar topics.

Whichever book is right for your reader, Blastoff! Readers are the perfect books to build confidence and encourage a love of reading that will last a lifetime!

This edition first published in 2019 by Bellwether Media, Inc.

Library of Congress Cataloging-in-Publication Data

Names: Pettiford, Rebecca, author.
Title: Collared Lemmings / by Rebecca Pettiford.
Description: Minneapolis, MN : Bellwether Media, Inc., 2019. |
   Series: Blastoff! Readers. Animals of the Arctic | Audience: Age 5-8. |
   Audience: K to Grade 3. | Includes bibliographical references and index.
Identifiers: LCCN 2018030960 (print) | LCCN 2018036175 (ebook) |
   ISBN 9781681036618 (ebook) | ISBN 9781626179363 (hardcover : alk. paper)
Subjects: LCSH: Collared lemming--Juvenile literature. | Animals--Arctic regions--Juvenile literature.
Classification: LCC QL737.R666 (ebook) | LCC QL737.R666 P44 2019 (print) | DDC 590.911--dc23
LC record available at https://lccn.loc.gov/2018030960

Editor: Rebecca Sabelko   Designer: Jeffrey Kollock

Printed in the United States of America, North Mankato, MN

Table of Contents

Collared lemmings are small **rodents**. They **burrow** through the snow of the Arctic **tundra**.

These animals love this cold, dry, and rocky **biome**.

Northern Collared Lemming Range

range = □

Collared lemmings have gray and brown fur that turns white each fall.

summer fur

winter fur ↙

Their thick fur matches the snow.
This **adaptation** helps them
hide from **predators**.

Collared lemmings have small ears.
They have short legs and tails, too.

Their small body parts
help them stay warm.

Collared lemmings grow long claws each winter. The claws are like snow shovels!

claws

Special Adaptations

small ears

thick fur

sharp claws

They use these sharp claws to dig up food under snow and ice.

Safe and Cozy

Collared lemmings stay safe in burrows. They dig their summer burrows right above the **permafrost**.

Sometimes, they hide under rocks to escape predators.

Northern Collared Lemming Stats

Least Concern	Near Threatened	Vulnerable	Endangered	Critically Endangered	Extinct in the Wild	Extinct

conservation status: least concern

life span: up to 3 years

13

In winter, they dig burrows
deep under the snow.
There, they make grass nests.

These warm homes keep lemmings safe from bears, foxes, and owls.

Collared lemmings eat many different plants. They have strong front teeth that never stop growing!

They chew on hard plants
to wear their teeth down.

Collared lemmings eat grasses, berries, and young plants during the summer.

In winter, they dig for twigs, bark, and willow buds.

Collared Lemming Diet

cotton grass

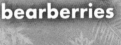
bearberries

willow buds

Collared lemmings spend about six hours a day looking for food.

They need a lot of **energy** to live in the tundra!

Glossary

adaptation—a change an animal undergoes over a long period of time to fit where it lives

biome—a large area with certain plants, animals, and weather; collared lemmings live in the Arctic tundra biome.

burrow—to dig holes or tunnels to live in

energy—the power to move and do things

permafrost—a thick layer of the ground that stays frozen all year

predators—animals that hunt other animals for food

rodents—small animals that gnaw on their food

tundra—rocky land in the Arctic that has a frozen layer of ground and little plant life

To Learn More

AT THE LIBRARY

Munro, Roxie. *Rodent Rascals*. New York, N.Y.:
Holiday House, 2018.

Phillips, Dee. *Collared Lemming*. New York, N.Y.:
Bearport Publishing, 2015.

Sill, Cathryn. *About Rodents: A Guide for Children*.
Atlanta, Ga.: Peachtree, 2016.

ON THE WEB

FACTSURFER

Factsurfer.com gives you
a safe, fun way to find
more information.

1. Go to www.factsurfer.com.

2. Enter "collared lemmings" into the search box.

3. Click the "Surf" button and select your book cover
   to see a list of related web sites.

Index

The images in this book are reproduced through the courtesy of: All Canada Photos/ Alamy, front cover (collared lemming); Jukka Jantunen, pp. 4-5; NHPA/ SuperStock, p. 6; Andrey Zvoznikov/Pantheon/ SuperStock, pp. 6-7, 11 (bubble), 17; Cordier Sylvain/Hemis/ SuperStock, pp. 8-9 (left); Tom McHugh/ Getty, pp. 8-9 (right cutout), 14-15, 16-17; All Canada Photos/ Alamy, pp. 10; 11, 12; Biosphoto/ Alamy, pp. 12-13, 22; Fabrice Simon/ Biosphoto, p. 15; Pierre Vernay/Polar Lys/ Biosphoto, pp. 18-19, 20-21, 21; Nicram Sabod, p. 19 (cotton grass); Alexey Svatov, p. 19 (bearberry); Slavikbig, p. 19 (willow buds).